PRAY TO BE OKAY

A Mother & Son's Invitation to Pray for Any and Everything

Written by Author J. LaStar
and Malachi Williams

Copyright © 2012 Author Name

All rights reserved.

ISBN: 978-0-578-31035-0

Pray to be ok

The Prayer of a King

Lord, I come to you today, asking you to guide me. I ask that you guide me as a king so that I may defend my castle in the best way possible. I ask that you may help me defend and provide for my family. God, I can't move without you, I need you to breathe through me, I need bm you to appear before I'm seen. God I humbly ask for you to reign and rule over me, mind, body, spirit, and soul. When I'm sad God only you can comfort me. When I'm lost I need you to see me through. God, I need you as I tie my tie and lace my shoes, because through you I will have the strength to be worthy enough to live as a king and teach others around me how to live like kings too. God I am unworthy, but I confess my sins, I confess my shortcomings and I ask for forgiveness, and I ask that you rip apart anything that does not represent my kingdom and you, and in your son Jesus name I pray, Amen

Pray to be ok

Pray to be ok

Prayer of a Queen

Lord take my hand, you've given me a path of a nurture, you've given me the power to hold life as you create, God stand with me when I am weak, Lord help me respond to every situation I come across on the path to do your will, with love and strength that can only come through you, Help me to forgive as you have forgiven me over and over again. Give me what's mine of gid, and I pray that my light is shown through your grace and your mercies. God when my crown is heavy or crooked, or one of my jewels falls to the ground I pray that you restore me to stand in the greatness and the power and the might to weather any storm. I pray that you get the glory from my story, and every task that I start with I finish no matter what. When I'm lonely I pray that I have the strength to turn to you, I repent for my shortcoming, I repent for my disobedience, and I repent for thinking I can do it all alone. You are the Almighty all seeing all knowing father and I pray that today and every day that I remember where my help comes from, Amen

Pray to be ok

Pray to be ok

A morning prayer for you.

God coming to you thanking you for this unpromised gift of life you've given. Thank you for your grace and mercies. Thank you for you love power and protection over me and my family through last night. Thank you for your sacrifice of death and for your forgiveness. I stand undeserving. God please create in me a clean heart. God as I stand forgiveness and healed in Jesus name I pray you would bless this day with purpose and focus. Help me to stand in your strength. Shine through me so my light can deter judgement from others, misery, and sin. God these things I ask as my day is started. In the name of Jesus I pray. Amen.

Pray to be ok

Pray to be ok

AFFIRMATIONS

Pray to be ok

Pray to be ok

Words of Affirmation for Men

No matter what anyone sees, I feel like a king, I am a king. I am capable of giving love. I deserve to be loved. I am responsible for my actions. My mental strength is the weapon I use to protect my heart and my soul. Being at my best will help me be there to love and protect my family. I do not need validation because I do not take my instruction or guidance from my peers. I love and respect myself and command everyone around me to do the same.

-Author J. LaStar

Pray to be ok

Words of Affirmation for Women

I love myself, respect myself and accept myself exactly as I am. My crown is made of grace, strength and fearlessness. I desire only what I deserve. I strive for equality, but I will not beg for attention. I am a queen. What's meant for me I will have.

– Author J. LaStar

Pray to be ok

Words of Affirmation for Kids and Teenagers

Learning is my super power. I can do the hard things. I am a problem solver. I am a leader. I choose my attitude. There is someone who loves me. I am a good friend. I strive to be personal not perfect. I will enjoy my whole life.

– Author J. LaStar

Pray to be ok

Pray to be ok

John 16:33

"I have said these things to you, that in me you may have peace. In the world you will have tribulation. But take heart; I have overcome the world."

Pray to be ok

My Peace

God, I see the things you do, and I thank you for everything you do both things we see and things we don't notice and I would like to come to you asking for peace among the world. I ask you to come and give people the mind to try and not cause any chaos for other people including themselves. I ask that you come into our minds and help us make the correct decisions to make the world a better place. In your son Jesus name, Amen.

Pray to be ok

Luke 10:27

And he answered, "You shall love the Lord your God with all your heart, and with all your soul, and with all your strength, and with all your mind; and your neighbor as yourself."

Pray to be ok

My Love for Mankind

God, you have displayed the ultimate example of what love looks like. Thank you for that example. Please teach me how to love unconditionally. I want to be able to see past the hurt and pain that is easy to see and feel in order to get to a place where I can exemplify the same love you have shown. Help me Lord. In Jesus name I pray, Amen.

Pray to be ok

John 15:10–12

"If you keep my commandments, you will abide in my love, just as I have kept my Father's commandments and abide in his love. These things I have spoken to you, that my joy may be in you, and that your joy may be full. 'This is my commandment, that you love one another as I have loved you.'"

Pray to be ok

My Joy

Lord, you told me that if I keep your commandments you will give me joy. God thank you for your promise. Thank you for giving me enough love to spread without losing love for myself. God your joy is what I desire and I thank you for giving me that gift. Please help me to remember I have your joy and everything will be alright. I have a reason to smile even when its dark in my life. I pray that you will bless those that seek your joy too. In your son Jesus name, Amen.

Pray to be ok

Psalm 37:4

Delight yourself in the Lord, and he will give you the desires of your heart.

Pray to be ok

My Pleasure

God I would like to thank you for being such a wonderful and forgiving god, I thank you for dying for our sins and I come to you to ask you to please help me to delight myself in you at all times. God I am chasing you in this life and I pray your fulfilled promises continuously renew my passion and keep me satisfied in you as I continue to trust and obey you according to scripture. Thank you for reading my heart. In Jesus name. Amen.

Pray to be ok

Exodus 20:12

"Honor your father and your mother, that your days may be long in the land that the Lord your God is giving you.

Pray to be ok

My Children

Lord I thank you for everything you do for not only just me but for everyone, I thank you for forgiving us when we do things that aren't pleasing to you, God I come to you asking for help, I ask that you bless my children and all the children of the world, I ask you to bless my children with safety and good maybe even great health, I ask you to bless them with long lives so that they may be here when I'm long gone, and I thank you for being such a wonderful and forgiving god and I pray in your son Jesus name, Amen.

Pray to be ok

1 Corinthians 12:28

And God has placed in the church first of all apostles, second prophets, third teachers, then miracles, then gifts of healing, of helping, of guidance, and of different kinds of tongues.

Pray to be ok

Asking For Guidance

Lord, I come to you today thanking you for your blessings and your lessons you teach us in your word, Lord I come to you for guidance. Lord I ask you for directions to be more like you Lord. I thank you for everything you've done for me. I ask you to come into my mind and guide me to the correct path. In your son Jesus name, Amen.

Pray to be ok

Luke 6:31

Do to others as you would have them do to you.

Pray to be ok

Gaining Friends

Lord, I come to you as humbly as I can thanking you for your grace and your mercy, I thank you for everything you do for us we thank you for your blessings and forgiveness. I come to you today asking you to bless me with friends. Lord I ask you to please send me some friends I can hang out with and be around. Lord I know you told me to treat others how I want to be treated and I'm working on it. I just ask that you send me people to talk to. In your son Jesus name I pray, Amen.

Pray to be ok

Psalm 127:3-5

Behold, children are a heritage from the Lord, the fruit of the womb a reward. Like arrows in the hand of a warrior are the children of one's youth. Blessed is the man who fills his quiver with them! He shall not be put to shame when he speaks with his enemies in the gate.

Pray to be ok

Expanding Family

Lord, I come to you today thanking you for being such a wonderful and forgiving god, and I thank you for all the strength you've given everyone your blessings, I ask that you bless us so we can expand our family, I ask that you bless us with more children to fill our homes and our hearts and in your son Jesus name I pray, Amen

Pray to be ok

Colossians 3:23

Whatever you do, work heartily, as for the Lord and not for men,

Pray to be ok

Gaining Passions

Lord I thank you for allowing me to be here today and I thank you for helping me when I need it and whenever I want it and don't ask for it, I come to you to ask that you help me find something I can be passionate about, I ask for your help to find something I can do with joy in my heart, I ask you to help me find something I can do that I'm great at and help me do it with passion, in your son Jesus name I pray, Amen.

Pray to be ok

Proverbs 31:10-12

An excellent wife who can find? She is far more precious than jewels. The heart of her husband trusts in her, and he will have no lack of gain. She does him good, and not harm, all the days of her life.

Pray to be ok

Gaining a Husband

God, I come to you today as humbly as I can, thanking you for not only the things you do for me but the things you do for the world, although everyone may not believe you are there I believe and see your work, I come to you today asking you for help, I ask that you help me find a husband that trusts me whole heartedly, I ask that you help me find a husband that does more good than harm, I ask that you make him a joy to be around and won't discourage my dreams, and in your son Jesus name I pray, Amen

Pray to be ok

Genesis 2:1

Then the Lord God said, "It is not good that the man should be alone; I will make him a helper fit for him."

Pray to be ok

Gaining a Wife

Lord, you are an oh so amazing god, you help everyone do things and nothing would be possible without you lord, I ask that you help me find a loving wife I can care for, I ask that you help me find someone that will love me for me and not my possessions, I ask that you send me someone that will take away my loneliness and turn that into happiness, and I pray in your son Jesus name, Amen.

Pray to be ok

Acts 9:31

So the church throughout all Judea and Galilee and Samaria had peace and was being built up. And walking in the fear of the Lord and in the comfort of the Holy Spirit, it multiplied.

Pray to be ok

Church Growth

God I come to you thanking you for helping me when I'm down and I thank you for everything you do even when we don't ask for it, I come to you asking for help with our church, I ask that you help me expand our church as much as possible, God we want to spread your word as much as possible and we just don't have a lot of members to do that, I ask that you put our church in people's minds that don't have a church home to go to, and in your son Jesus name I pray, Amen.

Pray to be ok

1 Corinthians 2:14

But the natural man receiveth not the things of the Spirit of God: for they are foolishness unto him: neither can he know them, because they are spiritually discerned.

Pray to be ok

Discernment

We thank you for healing us, healing our minds soul and body when we didn't have the strength to move lord and We need you God to invade our minds. Show me what I need to see in order to discern what guidance comes from your kingdom. I desire your will to be done for my life. Please give me more of you and less of me. I need to hear you. Show me how to position myself to receive you. There are situations that blind me and close my heart but I need you to breath into me Oh Lord. Day by Day in your son's mighty name, Amen.

Pray to be ok

Psalm 121:1-4

A Song of Ascents. I lift up my eyes to the hills. From where does my help come? My help comes from the Lord, who made heaven and earth. He will not let your foot be moved; he who keeps you will not slumber.

Pray to be ok

Business

God you give us life and we thank you for allowing us to be here on this earth living and breathing and I come to you today asking for help, I ask that you help my business grow and make more money, Lord I ask that you help us come up with ideas that will increase our sales, I thank you for being a forgiving and wonderful god and in your son Jesus name I pray, Amen.

Pray to be ok

2 Timothy 3:16

All Scripture is breathed out by God and profitable for teaching, for reproof, for correction, and for training in righteousness,

Pray to be ok

Spiritual Growth

God, I thank you for blessing me allowing me to wake up this morning. I don't deserve what you have given me. I thank you for being a faithful job. I ask that you please help my spiritual mind. I ask you to help me grow and help my mind mature, I ask that you teach me to be more like you God, I thank you for keeping me alive all this time, Lord and I really thank you for teaching me all that I've learned so far. Please forgive me for overlooking your power when I needed you to most. Thank you for loving me. In your son Jesus name I pray, Amen

Pray to be ok

Jeremiah 29:11

For I know the plans I have for you,
declares the Lord, plans for welfare and not
for evil, to give you a future and a hope.

Pray to be ok

Prosperity

God, I thank you for everything you've given me, I ask that you bless me with good fortune, God I ask that you put in motion whatever have in store for me, I ask that you bless me with good fortune and prosperity, and in your sone Jesus name I pray, Amen.

Pray to be ok

Matthew 21:22

And whatever you ask in prayer, you will receive, if you have faith."

Pray to be ok

Having more Faith

There has been some hard days over the past few years. We as a people have been blind to seeking ye first. God, I thank you for being an oh so amazing God in spite of and listening to everyone's prayers and helping us even when we do not ask. God I ask you send me to tell the message that the blood still works. I just ask that you help me find more faith in you. I believe that you sent your only son Jesus to die on the cross for our sins but Lord I want to learn through your teachings on how to believe in you with my whole heart body and soul. I ask that you guide me on the correct path to more faith in you and I ask that you help me find faith in the things you do for me and for everyone and in your son Jesus name I pray, Amen.

Pray to be ok

Proverbs 3:9-10

Honor the Lord with your wealth and with the first fruits of all your produce; then your barns will be filled with plenty, and your vats will be bursting with wine.

Pray to be ok

My Enlarge Territory

God you've been great to me, every step of the way even when I didn't deserve it. Thank you for that. Your word says if we ask, we shall receive according to your riches and glory. I need to grow my faith and my message. I come to ask you to bless me so that I can enlarge my territory. I ask that you help me, and in your son Jesus name I pray, Amen.

Pray to be ok

Acts 5:29

But Peter and the apostles answered, "We must obey God rather than men.

Pray to be ok

Staying Obedient

God I ask you to forgive me for not always being obedient. I ask that you speak louder in my head when you know I'm about to do something I don't have any business doing, I know that sometimes you may speak into my head telling me I shouldn't do this or I shouldn't do that and I ask that you may further help me resist my urges to keep doing the thing I'm not supposed to be, I ask that you give me a little bit of a push to get back on the right track, I ask that you help me stay obedient when I cannot and I ask that you give me the strength and mindset that I need to move forward in being more obedient and in your son Jesus name I pray, Amen.

Pray to be ok

Acts 3:19

Repent therefore, and turn again, that your sins may be blotted out,

Pray to be ok

Repenting for your sins

Lord you are my one and only god I serve you and no one else and I come to you today asking for forgiveness, I ask you to forgive me for doing the things I wasn't supposed to do and I ask you to forgive me for doing anything that wasn't pleasing to your all seeing eyes, I ask that you help me with your teachings in your word so that I may hope to be more like you, I ask that you may help me spread your word to others so that we may all commit fewer sins so that we may make the world a better place for all of us and in your son Jesus name I pray. Amen.

Pray to be ok

Proverbs 17:22

A joyful heart is good medicine, but a crushed spirit dries up the bones.

Pray to be ok

Better Health

This is your temple. God I know that you are my savior and you have been helping me and everyone else my whole life I thank you for the many years you have spent watching the world and everything on it I thank you for all the time you've spent helping not only me but everyone else and I come to you asking for help, I ask that you help me achieve better health, Lord I know I'm not where I'm supposed to be in my health, I ask that you may keep me on track with getting better health, I ask that you bless me with better health, and in your son Jesus name I pray, Amen.

Pray to be ok

Deuteronomy 31:6

Be strong and courageous. Do not fear or be in dread of them, for it is the Lord your God who goes with you. He will not leave you or forsake you."

Pray to be ok

My Strength

God, I come to you to thank you for the strength you've blessed me with and I thank you for the blessing you've given me so far and I thank you for all of the help you've given me with all my past problems and I ask that you may strengthen me so that I may be strong with you on my side, Lord I ask that you give me strength so that I may be strong with faith in you, in your son Jesus name I pray, Amen.

Pray to be ok

Romans 12:12

Rejoice in hope, be patient in tribulation, be constant in prayer.

Pray to be ok

Gaining Patience

God I would like to thank you for the patience you've given me to last me this long and I thank you for all of the things you do for all of us and I ask that you help me be more patient, I ask that you may give me more patience so that I may not cause any problems with anyone so that I may love thy neighbor and not get annoyed by them and in your son Jesus name I pray, Amen.

Pray to be ok

2 Thessalonians 3:10

For even when we were with you, we would give you this command: If anyone is not willing to work, let him not eat.

Pray to be ok

Getting a Job

Lord I see the work you do for me and I would like to thank you and I see that you always help me and others that have faith in you and I ask that you please bless me with a job opportunity, I ask that you give me a chance at a job so that I may always be able to have money in my pocket, I ask that you bless me with a chance with a job so that I may not have to worry about not having food, and in your son Jesus name I pray, Amen.

Pray to be ok

Isaiah 60:1

Arise, shine, for your light has come, and the glory of the Lord has risen upon you.

Pray to be ok

Let Your Light Shine

God, I thank you for being a loving and forgiving god even though we don't deserve it, but I ask you to let my light shine, I ask you to let people see and notice me, I ask you to let my light shine greater than it ever has before, and in your son Jesus name I pray, Amen.

Pray to be ok

Daniel 1:20

And in all matters of wisdom and understanding, that the king enquired of them, he found them ten times better than all the magicians and astrologers that were in all his realm.

Pray to be ok

Having a better Understanding

Lord I come to you thanking you for everything you've ever done for me, I thank you for helping me through everything, and lord I ask you to give me the wisdom I need to better understand people, I ask that you give me the wisdom I need to be more like you lord, and in your son Jesus name I pray, Amen.

Pray to be ok

Philippians 4:6-7

Do not be anxious about anything, but in everything by prayer and supplication with thanksgiving let your requests be made known to God. And the peace of God, which surpasses all understanding, will guard your hearts and your minds in Christ Jesus.

Pray to be ok

My Anxiety

Lord, I come to you today thanking you for everything you've done, not just for me but for everyone, and I ask that you help me with my anxiety, I ask that you calm my heart and my mind, I ask that you give me the confidence to keep myself cool calm and collected, and in your son Jesus name I pray, Amen.

Pray to be ok

Psalm 34:17-18

When the righteous cry for help, the Lord hears and delivers them out of all their troubles. The Lord is near to the brokenhearted and saves the crushed in spirit.

Pray to be ok

My Depression

Lord I come to you thanking you for everything and everyone in my life, and I come to you asking you to help me with my depression, I ask you to help me with all my troubles, I ask you to help me get better and help me fix my mind, I ask you to save me from my sadness, and in your son Jesus name I pray, Amen

Pray to be ok

John 16:33

I have said these things to you, that in me you may have peace. In the world you will have tribulation. But take heart; I have overcome the world."

Pray to be ok

Their Peace

Lord, I come to you asking you to bless my oved ones with peace, I ask you to bring peace to their mind, I ask that you give them the mindset of only causing peace, and in you son Jesus name I pray, Amen.

Pray to be ok

John 3:16

"For God so loved the world, that he gave his only Son, that whoever believes in him should not perish but have eternal life.

Pray to be ok

A Family/Friend to find love

God, I come to you today thanking you for everything you've done for me and I come asking you for a loved one to find love, I ask that you find them someone who can make them feel wanted and appreciated, I ask that you find them someone they can love and cherish, and in you son Jesus name I pray, Amen

Pray to be ok

Romans 15:13

May the God of hope fill you with all joy and peace in believing, so that by the power of the Holy Spirit you may abound in hope.

Pray to be ok

Their Joy

Lord, I thank you for so forgiving and loving when we don't deserve it Lord, but I come to you asking for joy for my loved one, I ask that you may bring them unimaginable joy, I pray that you make them happy and full of joy, and in your son Jesus name I pray, Amen

Pray to be ok

Proverbs 21:17

Whoever loves pleasure will be a poor man;
he who loves wine and oil will not be rich.

Pray to be ok

Their Pleasure

Lord I ask that you bless my loved one with pleasure, I ask that you give them pleasure in what they enjoy to do, I ask that you allow them to enjoy their everyday activities, I also ask that you give them happiness in their everyday life, and in your son Jesus name I pray, Amen

Pray to be ok

Ephesians 6:4

Fathers, do not provoke your children to anger, but bring them up in the discipline and instruction of the Lord.

Pray to be ok

For the Children of the world

Lord, I pray for all the children of the world. I prau that they all have homes to go to. I pray that they all have loving friends and family members that protects them. I pray they all stay safe. I pray that you may guide them and protect them so they may live a long and good life. In Jesus Name, Amen.

Pray to be ok

Proverbs 3:5-6

Trust in the Lord with all your heart, and do not lean on your own understanding. In all your ways acknowledge him, and he will make straight your paths.

Pray to be ok

Guidance for others

God, I thank you for everything you've given me, I ask that you bless others with guidance, I ask that you may help them in their time of need, and in your sone Jesus name I pray, Amen.

Pray to be ok

2 Thessalonians 3:3

But the Lord is faithful. He will establish you and guard you against the evil one.

Pray to be ok

My Protection

Lord, I come to you asking you for protection. I pray that you wrap me in your arms. I'm sorry for putting myself in situations I can't get out of, please protect me from my bad decisions. Lord I ask that you keep others from being harmed from bad decisions. Thank you Lord, for keeping my family and friends this far. We don't deserve your grace but I thank you for it any. In Jesus name I pray. Amen.

Pray to be ok

Psalm 91:1-16

He who dwells in the shelter of the Most High will abide in the shadow of the Almighty. I will say to the Lord, "My refuge and my fortress, my God, in whom I trust." For he will deliver you from the snare of the fowler and from the deadly pestilence. He will cover you with his pinions, and under his wings you will find refuge; his faithfulness is a shield and buckler.

Pray to be ok

Family's Protection

God, you are our one and only god, I come to you today asking you for protection for my family, I ask you to protect us from any dangers to come, and I ask that you please keep us safe, we also ask that you keep our far away family safe, and in you son Jesus name we pray, Amen.

Pray to be ok

Isaiah 41:10

Fear not, for I am with you; be not dismayed, for I am your God; I will strengthen you, I will help you, I will uphold you with my righteous right hand.

Pray to be ok

Protection for Friends

God, I come to you asking you for protection for my friends, I ask you to guide them to safety, I pray that you may protect them, I pray that you may keep them from danger, and I ask that you may keep them out of trouble, and in your son Jesus name I pray, Amen

Pray to be ok

Nehemiah 13:2

Because they met not the children of Israel with bread and with water, but hired Balaam against them, that he should curse them: howbeit our God turned the curse into a blessing.

Pray to be ok

A Woman who want's children

Lord I thank you for allowing me to be here today, I thank you for me having a place to sleep at night, I thank you for everything you've done when I needed you most and even the times when I didn't thank you for the things you've given me, and I come to you to pray for the families that are wanting children, I ask that you may bless them with a child or children, and in your son Jesus name I pray, Amen

Pray to be ok

Acts 1:3

To whom also he shewed himself alive after his passion by many infallible proofs, being seen of them forty days, and speaking of the things pertaining to the kingdom of God:

Pray to be ok

Finding your passions

Lord, I come to you thanking you because you as my lord and savior have helped me so many times throughout my life and I can't thank you enough for everything you've done for me, and I come asking you to bless me to find my passions, I ask that you bless me so I can find things I can be passionate about, and in your son Jesus name I pray, Amen

Pray to be ok

Genesis 43:28

And they answered, Thy servant our father is in good health, he is yet alive. And they bowed down their heads, and made obeisance.

Pray to be ok

Their Health

Lord, I thank you for allowing me to be here today, I thank you for everyone in my life, I come to you asking for their health, I ask that you bless them with good health, I ask that you please bless them with a great long life, and in your son Jesus name I pray, Amen

Pray to be ok

2 John 1:9

Everyone who goes on ahead and does not abide in the teaching of Christ, does not have God. Whoever abides in the teaching has both the Father and the Son.

Pray to be ok

Finding a Church Home

God, I come to you asking for your help with finding a church home, Lord I ask that you may help me find a church home so that I may enlighten not only myself and my family with your teachings, I ask that you may further expand my knowledge with the people who have studied your word and are willing to teach others so that they may share your knowledge and wisdom with the world, and we thank you for the things you do even though sometimes we may not thank you but we thank you and in your son Jesus name I pray, Amen

Pray to be ok

2 Samuel 19:6

In that thou lovest thine enemies, and hatest thy friends. For thou hast declared this day, that thou regards neither princes nor servants: for this day I perceive, that if Absalom had lived, and all we had died this day, then it had pleased thee well.

Pray to be ok

A friend to have

God you have told us to love thy neighbor and treat others how we want to be treated, We love you and praise you for everything you do for us, I ask you to bless me with friends to have and to be around, I ask that you may bless me with friends to make plans with and be around, and in your son Jesus name I pray, Amen

Pray to be ok

1 Kings 16:11

And it came to pass, when he began to reign, as soon as he sat on his throne, that he slew all the house of Baasha: he left him not one that pisseth against a wall, neither of his kinsfolks, nor of his friends.

Pray to be ok

Gaining more Friends

God you have told us to love thy neighbor and treat others how we want to be treated, We love you and praise you for everything you do for us, I ask you to bless me with friends to have and to be around, I ask that you may bless me with friends to make plans with and be around, and in your son Jesus name I pray, Amen

Pray to be ok

Hosea 9:7

The days of visitation are come, the days of recompence are come; Israel shall know it: the prophet is a fool, the spiritual man is mad, for the multitude of thine iniquity, and the great hatred.

Pray to be ok

Their Spiritual Growth

God, we all see you as a wonderful god, and we known that you are our savior, I pray that you may help their spiritual growth, I ask that you make help them become more open minded and in your son Jesus name I pray, Amen

Pray to be ok

Romans 8:5-6

For they that are after the flesh do mind the things of the flesh; but they that are after the Spirit the things of the Spirit. For to be carnally minded is death; but to be spiritually minded is life and peace.

Pray to be ok

Their mind to Prosper

God, I come to you today thanking you, I thank you for the air we all breathe, I thank you for the food I eat, and I come to you asking you to help their mind prosper, I ask that you may help them come up with things that will help them, and in your son Jesus name I pray, Amen

Pray to be ok

Hebrews 11

Now faith is the substance of things hoped for, the evidence of things not seen. For by it the elders obtained a good report. Through faith we understand that the worlds were framed by the word of God, so that things which are seen were not made of things which do appear.

Pray to be ok

Them to Have Faith

Lord, I come to you today asking you to guide me. Lord as your all seeing eyes may have seen I haven't been feeling too happy lately. I ask that you guide me to happiness. Lord I pray that you rebuke the enemy's shots against me. I rebuke all things that hinders all of us from the things you try to give us. I ask that you speak louder into our heads when the devil tempts us to stray further away from you. We thank you for being a faithful God and in your son Jesus' name I pray. Amen.

Pray to be ok

Proverbs 13:11

Dishonest money dwindles away, but whoever gathers money little by little makes it grow.

Pray to be ok

Their Financial Growth

Lord, I come to you today asking you to guide me. Lord as your all seeing eyes may have seen I haven't been feeling too happy lately. I ask that you guide me to happiness. Lord I pray that you rebuke the enemy's shots against me. I rebuke all things that hinders all of us from the things you try to give us. I ask that you speak louder into our heads when the devil tempts us to stray further away from you. We thank you for being a faithful God and in your son Jesus' name I pray. Amen.

Pray to be ok

1 Samuel 15:22

And Samuel said, Hath the Lord as great delight in burnt offerings and sacrifices, as in obeying the voice of the Lord? Behold, to obey is better than sacrifice, and to hearken than the fat of rams.

Pray to be ok

Their Obedience

Lord, I come to you today asking for you to help me spread the word about our obedience. I ask you to help them stay on track and do the right things, and in your son Jesus name I pray, Amen

Pray to be ok

Colossians 1:14

In whom we have redemption through his blood, even the forgiveness of sins:

Pray to be ok

A Friend to Forgive themselves

God I ask you to forgive me for not always being obedient, I ask that you speak louder in my head when you know I'm about to do something I don't have any business doing, I ask that you help me stay obedient when I cannot, and in your son Jesus name I pray, Amen

Pray to be ok

Luke 18:15-17

And they brought unto him also infants, that he would touch them: but when his disciples saw it, they rebuked them. But Jesus called them unto him, and said, Suffer little children to come unto me, and forbid them not: for of such is the kingdom of God. Verily I say unto you, Whosoever shall not receive the kingdom of God as a little child shall in no wise enter therein.

Pray to be ok

Foster Care Children

God there are children in this world that need good homes. I ask you send the help those children need. Make me available for those children that are in need. Teach me how to love even in difficult times. Help me be an example of tolerance and patience. God let your will be done on earth as it is in Heaven in your son Jesus name. Amen

Pray to be ok

Deuteronomy 31:6

Be strong and of a good courage, fear not, nor be afraid of them: for the Lord thy God, he it is that doth go with thee; he will not fail thee, nor forsake thee.

Pray to be ok

Courage

God, I come to thank you for the blessings you've given all of us and I thank you for keeping me here on this earth and I ask that you may bless us all with more life, Lord I come to you today asking you to help me, I ask that you help me gain the courage to take that final leap of faith. I ask that you may fill me with the courage I need to get away from the things that hold me back and I thank you for being such a wonderful and forgiving god and I pray in your son Jesus name, Amen.

Pray to be ok

Luke 5:15

But so much the more went there a fame abroad of him: and great multitudes came together to hear, and to be healed by him of their infirmities.

Pray to be ok

Healing

Lord, I thank you for being an oh so amazing god, and I thank you for helping me when I ask you to and even when I don't ask and you still help, I ask that you come to me and heal me and all the people of the earth lord, I haven't really been myself in these past few days and I ask that you may heal me and return me to my normal self, I pray to you asking you to heal all the people that are in the hospital, I ask that you help all the people around the world, and in your son Jesus name I pray, Amen.

Pray to be ok

Matthew 11:28

Come to me, all you who are weary and burdened, and I will give you rest.

Pray to be ok

Their Healing

Lord, I thank you for being an oh so amazing god, and I thank you for helping me when I ask you and even when I don't ask and you still help, I ask that you come to me and heal me lord, I haven't really been myself in these past few days and I ask that you may heal me and return me to my normal self, and in your son Jesus name I pray, Amen.

Pray to be ok

2 John 1:9

Everyone who goes on ahead and does not abide in the teaching of Christ, does not have God. Whoever abides in the teaching has both the Father and the Son.

Pray to be ok

Healing of your mind

God, I come to you today asking you to help me ask that you heal my mind, I ask that you come into my mind and heal me, I ask that you may purify my mind and heal my mind, and heal my spirit, and in your son Jesus name I pray, Amen

Pray to be ok

Matthew 11:28

Come to me, all you who are weary and burdened, and I will give you rest.

Pray to be ok

Find a Friend a Church Home

God I come to you asking for help with our church, I ask that you help me expand our church as much as possible, God we want to spread your word as much as possible and we just don't have a lot of members to do that, I ask that you put our church in people's minds that don't have a church home to go to, and in your son Jesus name I pray, Amen

Pray to be ok

Romans 8:28

And we know that all things work together for good to them that love God, to them who are the called according to his purpose.

Pray to be ok

Their Healing of their mind

God, I come to you today asking you to help me ask that you heal my mind, I ask that you come into my mind and heal me, I ask that you may purify my mind and heal my mind, and heal my spirit, and in your son Jesus name I pray, Amen

Pray to be ok

1 Kings 5:5

And, behold, I purpose to build an house unto the name of the Lord my God, as the Lord spake unto David my father, saying, Thy son, whom I will set upon thy throne in thy room, he shall build an house unto my name.

Pray to be ok

Finding My Purpose

Lord, I ask that you please help me find my purpose, I ask that you help me find what I'm supposed to be doing with my life, I ask that you help me find out what I can do to help the world, and in your son Jesus name I pray, Amen

Pray to be ok

1 John 1:9

And, behold, I purpose to build an house unto the name of the Lord my God, as the Lord spake unto David my father, saying, Thy son, whom I will set upon thy throne in thy room, he shall build an house unto my name.

Pray to be ok

Finding Their Purpose

God, I thank you for everything you do for me and I ask that you please help them find their purpose, I ask that you please help them find their way, and in your son Jesus name I pray, Amen

Pray to be ok

Leviticus 16:34

And this shall be an everlasting statute unto you, to make an atonement for the children of Israel for all their sins once a year. And he did as the Lord commanded Moses.

Pray to be ok

Repenting for others sins

Lord, you told me that if I keep your commandments you will give me joy. God thank you for your promise. Thank you for giving me enough love to spread without losing love for myself. God your joy is what I desire and I thank you for giving me that gift. Please help me to remember I have your joy and everything will be alright. I have a reason to smile even when its dark in my life. I pray that you will bless those that seek your joy too. In your son Jesus name, Amen.

Pray to be ok

Leviticus 16:21

And Aaron shall lay both his hands upon the head of the live goat, and confess over him all the iniquities of the children of Israel, and all their transgressions in all their sins, putting them upon the head of the goat, and shall send him away by the hand of a fit man into the wilderness:

Pray to be ok

Asking For Guidance to Forgive yourself

Lord, I come to you today asking for forgiveness, I ask you to forgive me for doing anything that wasn't pleasing to your all seeing eyes. I ask you to forgive me for the things I've done that I wasn't supposed to and I ask you to please give me guidance on how to forgive myself, and in your son Jesus name I pray. Amen.

Pray to be ok

1 Corinthians 13

Though I speak with the tongues of men and of angels, and have not charity, I am become as sounding brass, or a tinkling cymbal. And though I have the gift of prophecy, and understand all mysteries, and all knowledge; and though I have all faith, so that I could remove mountains, and have not charity, I am nothing. And though I bestow all my goods to feed the poor, and though I give my body to be burned, and have not charity, it profited me nothing.

Pray to be ok

Helping a Friend Forgive Themselves

Lord, I come to you today asking for forgiveness, I ask you to forgive them for doing anything that wasn't pleasing to your all seeing eyes. I ask you to forgive them for the things they've done that they wasn't supposed to and in your son Jesus name I pray. Amen.

Pray to be ok

Isaiah 40:29

He giveth power to the faint; and to them that have no might he increased strength.

Pray to be ok

Finding strength to love again

Lord, I thank you for all that you do but I come to you in a not so good state, I ask that you help me find the strength to love again, I ask you to guide me in your teachings to find the courage and hope to find for someone to love again, I ask that you may help me find someone good for me not only financially but good for my mental health too, and in your son Jesus name I pray, Amen.

Pray to be ok

James 1:2-8

My brethren, count it all joy when ye fall into divers temptations; Knowing this, that the trying of your faith worketh patience. But let patience have her perfect work, that ye may be perfect and entire, wanting nothing.

Pray to be ok

Gaining strength to overcome something

Lord, I would like to sincerely thank you for everything you do for not only me but for everyone in the entire world, I thank you for your blessings and your forgiveness, and I ask that you may please bless me with your strength so that I may overcome my problems with great power and I ask that you lend me the knowledge so that I may be smart about it, and in your son Jesus name I pray, Amen.

Pray to be ok

Job 40

Moreover the Lord answered Job, and said, Shall he that contended with the Almighty instruct him? he that reproved God, let him answer it. Then Job answered the Lord,

Pray to be ok

Their Patience

Lord, as you are constantly watching us and caring for us, I would like to take a moment to thank you for what you do, I would like to thank you for allowing me to wake up another day and be here praising you, and I would like to ask for you help lord, I ask that you may help this person with their patience, and in your son Jesus name I pray, Amen.

Pray to be ok

Genesis 1:15

And let them be for lights in the firmament of the heaven to give light upon the earth: and it was so.

Pray to be ok

A Career For Them

Lord I come to you today, thanking you for everything you've done for everyone and everything. Although some of those things may not believe in you but I ask that you accept my thanks on behalf of them, and Lord I ask that you help them get a career and I ask that you allow them to be good at what they do, I ask that you may help them and teach them and in your son Jesus name I pray, Amen

Pray to be ok

Isaiah 60

Arise, shine; for thy light is come, and the glory of the Lord is risen upon thee. For, behold, the darkness shall cover the earth, and gross darkness the people: but the Lord shall arise upon thee, and his glory shall be seen upon thee. And the Gentiles shall come to thy light, and kings to the brightness of thy rising.

Pray to be ok

A Job for Them

Lord, I would like to thank you on behalf of everyone, we see what you do and we thank you for it, but I would like to ask you to help them get a job, I ask that you help them get a job so they can progress financially, I ask that you help them earn the things they need and want, and in your son Jesus name I pray, Amen.

Pray to be ok

1 Corinthians 14:40

Let all things be done decently and in order.

Pray to be ok

For them to shine

Lord I come to you today asking you to let them shine, I ask that you allow people to notice them, I ask that you allow them to strive in what they do, and in your son Jesus name I pray, Amen

Pray to be ok

Genesis 8:21

And the Lord smelled a sweet savior; and the Lord said in his heart, I will not again curse the ground any more for man's sake; for the imagination of man's heart is evil from his youth; neither will I again smite any more everything living, as I have done.

Pray to be ok

Having more Order and Decency

Lord I come to you to ask you for help, I ask that you bless me to do thing more orderly and efficiently, I ask that you help me organize things better so I can have everything in place, and in your son Jesus name I pray, Amen

Pray to be ok

Genesis 8:21

And the Lord smelled a sweet savior; and the Lord said in his heart, I will not again curse the ground any more for man's sake; for the imagination of man's heart is evil from his youth; neither will I again smite any more everything living, as I have done.

Pray to be ok

A Heart of Adah

Lord, I come to you today asking you to guide me to have a heart like Adah, I ask you to make me strong, I ask you to give me the power to overcome things even that are out of my control, I ask you to help me be more like you, and in your son Jesus name I pray, Amen

Pray to be ok

Genesis 6:5

And God saw that the wickedness of man was great in the earth, and that every imagination of the thoughts of his heart was only evil continually.

Pray to be ok

Having a Heart like Ruth

Lord I ask you to guide me to have a heart like ruth, I ask you to help me remove all of the toxins of evil and make them better, I ask that you help me be where I need to be, and in your son Jesus name I pray, Amen

Pray to be ok

Genesis 6:6

And it repented the Lord that he had made man on the earth, and it grieved him at his heart.

Pray to be ok

Having a Heart like Martha

Lord I come to you praying to you asking you to help me have a heart like Martha, I ask you to help me be free from temptation, I ask you to help me be free from evil, and in your son Jesus name I pray, Amen

Pray to be ok

Genesis 17:17

Then Abraham fell upon his face, and laughed, and said in his heart, Shall a child be born unto him that is an hundred years old? and shall Sarah, that is ninety years old, bear?

Pray to be ok

Having a Heart like Electa

God I come to you asking you to guide me to have a heart like electa, I ask you to fill me with joy, I ask that you bless me and my children with a long and fulling life, I ask that you help me be strong in the face of danger, and in your son Jesus name I pray, Amen

Pray to be ok

Genesis 18:5

And I will fetch a morsel of bread, and comfort ye your hearts; after that ye shall pass on: for therefore are ye come to your servant. And they said, So do, as thou hast said.

Pray to be ok

Having a Heart like Ester

God I come to you asking you to guide me to have a heart like Ester, I ask you to fill me with joy, I ask that you bless me and my children with a long and fulling life, I ask that you help me be strong in the face of danger, and in your son Jesus name I pray, Amen

Pray to be ok

Genesis 19:12

And the men said unto Lot, Hast thou here any besides? son in law, and thy sons, and thy daughters, and whatsoever thou hast in the city, bring them out of this place

Pray to be ok

Law Enforcement

Lord I come to you today asking you to help law enforcement, I ask that you may allow them to see the error of their ways, I ask that you may help them stay alive while keeping all of us safe, and in your son Jesus name I pray, Amen

Pray to be ok

Genesis 23:8

And he communed with them, saying, If it be your mind that I should bury my dead out of my sight; hear me, and intreat for me to Ephron the son of Zohar,

Pray to be ok

Having a Piece of Mind

Lord I ask you to help me have peace, I ask you to help me create a space in my mind that is only for peace, I ask that you please help me stay positive and peaceful, and in your Jesus name I pray, Amen

Pray to be ok

Matthew 5:43-48

Ye have heard that it hath been said, Thou shalt love thy neighbour, and hate thine enemy. But I say unto you, Love your enemies, bless them that curse you, do good to them that hate you, and pray for them which despitefully use you, and persecute you; That ye may be the children of your Father which is in heaven: for he maketh his sun to rise on the evil and on the good, and sendeth rain on the just and on the unjust.

Pray to be ok

Praying for your Enemies

Lord, I come to you today asking you to please keep my enemies safe, I ask that you may keep them out of danger, I ask that you may allow them to see the error of their ways, I ask that you may help them be nicer, and in your son Jesus name I pray, Amen

Pray to be ok

2 Corinthians 10

Now I Paul myself beseech you by the meekness and gentleness of Christ, who in presence am base among you, but being absent am bold toward you: But I beseech you, that I may not be bold when I am present with that confidence, wherewith I think to be bold against some, which think of us as if we walked according to the flesh. For though we walk in the flesh, we do not war after the flesh

Pray to be ok

Prayers for Yourself

Heavenly Father, thank you for being my peace. Thank you for bringing me through every storm you have. Thank you for walking me through the fire. You are worthy of all the praise. God help me find the next level in my life. Guide me to the thing I am supposed to do that brings me pleasure. That thing that brings me out of myself and into your grace. Like only you can. Please God help me find what pleasures me. In the mighty name of Jesus I am depending on you to show me what's next. Amen.

Pray to be ok

Psalm 37:4

Delight thyself also in the Lord and he shall give thee the desires of thine heart.

Pray to be ok

For your Happiness

Lord, I come to you today asking you to guide me. Lord as your all seeing eyes may have seen I haven't been feeling too happy lately. I ask that you guide me to happiness. Lord I pray that you rebuke the enemy's shots against me. I rebuke all things that hinders all of us from the things you try to give us. I ask that you speak louder into our heads when the devil tempts us to stray further away from you. We thank you for being a faithful God and in your son Jesus' name I pray. Amen.

Pray to be ok

Psalm 37:4

Delight thyself also in the Lord and he shall give thee the desires of thine heart.

Pray to be ok

Their Happiness

Lord, I come to you today asking you to guide me. Lord as your all seeing eyes may have seen I haven't been feeling too happy lately. I ask that you guide me to happiness. Lord I pray that you rebuke the enemy's shots against me. I rebuke all things that hinders all of us from the things you try to give us. I ask that you speak louder into our heads when the devil tempts us to stay further away from you. We thank you for being a faithful God and in your son Jesus' name I pray. Amen.

Pray to be ok

Jeremiah 14:19

Hast thou utterly rejected Judah? hath thy soul lothed Zion? why hast thou smitten us, and there is no healing for us? we looked for peace, and there is no good; and for the time of healing, and behold trouble!

Pray to be ok

Healing the sick

Lord my God, I come to you asking you for your healing power to come down on us. I ask that you heal those in need. I ask that you touch those who are sick in their minds. I pray for their safety. Please keep them from getting worse. I pray that you may give them the strength that only you can to get them through the hard times. Strengthen their immune systems. In your son's name, I am standing in the gap asking for healing and deliverance. Amen.

Pray to be ok

Luke 5:17

And it came to pass on a certain day, as he was teaching, that there were Pharisees and doctors of the law sitting by, which were come out of every town of Galilee, and Judaea, and Jerusalem: and the power of the Lord was present to heal them.

Pray to be ok

Helping the Nurses

Lord, I come to you today, thanking you for all that you do for not only make but for everyone , I thank you for all the things we notice And all the things we don't notice and the things we don't notice, I thank you for all the things you do for us but I come to you today asking you to please help the nurses while their helping the doctors, I ask that you keep them focused and ready for anything, and in your son Jesus name I pray, Amen

Pray to be ok

Luke 2:46

And it came to pass, that after three days they found him in the temple, sitting in the midst of the doctors, both hearing them, and asking them questions.

Pray to be ok

Helping the Doctors

Lord, I come to you today thanking you for everything you do, I thank you for that time you helped me last week and yesterday, and I thank you for helping me throughout my whole life so far, and I come to you asking you to help the doctors, I ask that you help them with the surgeries that they do, I ask that you help them stay focused and ready for anything, and in your son Jesus name I pray, Amen

Pray to be ok

Genesis 18:19

For I know him, that he will command his children and his household after him, and they shall keep the way of the Lord, to do justice and judgment; that the Lord may bring upon Abraham that which he hath spoken of him.

Pray to be ok

Helping the Judges Judgement

God, we see you as an all seeing god, we all see you as our lord and savior, and we come to you today asking you to help the judges stay focused and make the right decisions, we ask that you help their judgment not be clouded by personal favor and in your son Jesus name I pray, Amen

Pray to be ok

Luke 22:26

But ye shall not be so: but he that is greatest among you, let him be as the younger; and he that is chief, as he that doth serve.

Pray to be ok

Helping the President

Lord we come to you today asking you to help the president with their studies, I ask you to please help them make decisions that will make the world a better place, I ask that you fill them with the knowledge to get through situations that may endanger the world, and in your son Jesus name I pray, Amen

Pray to be ok

Philippians 2:6

Who, being in the form of God, thought it not robbery to be equal with God:

Pray to be ok

Equality for Everyone

Lord, I come to you today thanking you for the kindness you show everyone, and I ask that you help everyone gain true equality for all, Lord I ask that you help us be kinder to one another, and in your son Jesus name I pray, Amen

Pray to be ok

Lamentations 3:22-23

It is of the Lord's mercies that we are not consumed, because his compassions fail not. They are new every morning: great is thy faithfulness.

Pray to be ok

Remembering to Pray in the Morning

Lord, I ask that you please help me remember to pray in the morning, I ask that you help me remember all the things I have to do tomorrow, and in your son Jesus name I pray, Amen

Pray to be ok

Esther 6

On that night could not the king sleep, and he commanded to bring the book of records of the chronicles; and they were read before the king. And it was found written, that Mordecai had told of Bigthana and Teresh, two of the king's chamberlains, the keepers of the door, who sought to lay hand on the king Ahasuerus. And the king said, What honour and dignity hath been done to Mordecai for this? Then said the king's servants that ministered unto him, There is nothing done for him. ...

Pray to be ok

Remembering to Pray before sleeping

Lord, today I didn't get it all right and I hadn't get it all wrong. I need you to help me through the night so I can try it all again tomorrow.

Pray to be ok

Genesis 9:3

Every moving thing that liveth shall be meat for you; even as the green herb have I given you all things.

Pray to be ok

Payer over the Food

God, I come to you today, thanking for this food, I ask that you please bless the hands that prepared this food, and I ask that you please bless me with much more food to come, I ask that you please bless me so I won't have to worry about if I'll have enough food for me and my family, and in your son Jesus name I pray, Amen

Pray to be ok

Genesis 24:43

Behold, I stand by the well of water; and it shall come to pass, that when the virgin cometh forth to draw water, and I say to her, Give me, I pray thee, a little water of thy pitcher to drink

Pray to be ok

Prayer for your virginity

Lord, I come to you today thanking you for all the things that you do, Lord we all know that there are so many things you do for us each and everyday, not only for me but for all of us, we thank you for the things that you do that we both notice and don't notice, we thank you for the things you do without us asking and praying to you for, and lord I just ask that you help keep me pure for as long as you see fit, and in your son Jesus name I pray, Amen.

Pray to be ok

Leviticus 25:10

And ye shall hallow the fiftieth year, and proclaim liberty throughout all the land unto all the inhabitants thereof: it shall be a jubile unto you; and ye shall return every man unto his possession, and ye shall return every man unto his family.

Pray to be ok

Prayer for Grandparents

Lord I come to you thanking you for being a loving and forgiving god to all of us even though we don't deserve it, Lord I ask that you bless my grandparents with good health, Lord I ask that you bless them with many more years to their lives so that we may make as many memories with them as possible and I pay that you keep them from any dangers that may come, and in your son Jesus name I pray, Amen

Pray to be ok

Leviticus 20:5

Then I will set my face against that man, and against his family, and will cut him off, and all that go a whoring after him, to commit whoredom with Molech, from among their people.

Pray to be ok

Prayer for distant relatives

Lord, I come to you today thanking you for my family, and lord I ask that you protect everyone in my family, and I ask that you keep us safe, and lord I ask that you protect all of our distant family, I ask that you make sure their ok, and lord I ask that you protect all of my distant relatives, and In your son Jesus name I pray Amen.

Pray to be ok

Pray to be ok

PRAYERS CAN BE FUNNY BUT TRUE TOO

Pray to be ok

Pray to be ok

Finding my Keys

Lord I come to you asking you to help me find my keys, I need to go out and get something for the house, well really I just want to get out the house and find my keys and go somewhere covid has been rough for everyone and in your son Jesus name I pray, Amen

Pray to be ok

Finishing your text at a red light

Lord I ask that you let me finish my text that I'm about to send because I want to get across the street on time so I don't get caught at another red light I also don't want to get honked at because I'm texting at a red light, in your son Jesus name I pray, Amen.

Pray to be ok

Getting a stain out of a white shirt

Ok lord I come to you asking you to help me with this stain in my band new shirt, I need this shirt to wear today, and I just ask that you hep me get it out even though I was stupid enough to eat a hot dog with mustard with my new shirt on, I ask that you help me get the stain out and in you son Jesus name I pay, Amen.

Pray to be ok

Making it to work on time

Lord, I know what I have done for the past 15-20 minutes wasting my time when I'm supposed to be at least heading out the door but I was still in my bed wanting to go back to sleep, I actually thought about calling in sick but I ask that you please help me make it into work on time, Lord I would like to apologize for laying around and watching tv, I ask that you make all the cops get distracted for just enough time for me to speed past them to get to work and in your son Jesus name I pray, Amen.

Pray to be ok

Making the spider stay gone

Lord, let's just face it you know why I'm here, You know why I'm in a corner scared for my life right now, I don't even want to think about it but I have to because I want this STUPID SPIDER GO AWAY, and I just need you to do something with it, I don't care what you do with it or where it goes just make it go away from me and my house, please and thank you

Pray to be ok

Brining the gas station to you

Lord, I come to you desperately in need for something that is really really really super duper important, I ask that you please please please please bring that one gas station to me, you know that one gas station that's down the street I need you to bring me the whole gas station to me because I'm basically out of gas and didn't stop there this morning, Lord I know I should've stopped by this morning but I was scrolling through YouTube looking for a song to drive to work, Anyways I just need you to bring it to me so I can make home so I need you to just bring that to me please and thanks!

Pray to be ok

A working Microwave

Lord I ask you to bless me with a deal on a working microwave, I ask you to bless me with a way to have a working microwave, Lord I ask that you please allow me to have one so that I may heat up my food, and in your son Jesus name I pray, Amen

Pray to be ok

Make the coworker stop talking

Lord, I come to you thanking you for allowing me to be here today but I come to you to ask you for something, I ask that you please make my coworker stop talking, Lord I know you tell us to love thy neighbor and treat others how you want to be treated but I really just want this person to STOP TALKING, and lord I ask that you please quiet them down and in your son Jesus name I pray, Amen

Pray to be ok

No one hear me Fart

Lord, By now you probably already know why I'm here, Yes lord I did fart even though I just claimed I didn't know who farted and where it came from and I would like to apologize for that but I ask you that you please distract everyone from the smell of my fart and make them forget about it because lord I don't want to get made fun of because I farted in the middle of class during a test, In you son Jesus name I pray, Amen.

Pray to be ok

Keep my phone alive until the end of the day

Lord I come to you in my desperate time of need, I'm going to get straight to the point because I don't have much time left, Lord I need you to keep my phone alive until I can find a charger to charge it, Lord I'm super bored right now and I need you to keep my phone alive so I don't die of boredom, Lord I really need to keep scrolling on Facebook to be entertained with other peoples lives because the situation I'm in is super duper boring right now and I can't bare to be without Facebook for a few hours, In your son Jesus name I pray to you begging you to grant my prayer, Amen

Pray to be ok

Pray to be ok

About the Authors

Pray to be ok

Mom, Author J. LaStar grew up Church of God in Christ. The son Malachi have been raised Baptist. The family converted before Malachi was born in 2006. Prayer is a strong belief and reading the bible is important. Both Authors go through life daily believing that God is with them. Both authors never forget to thank God for their lives each and every day. Both Authors tend to Pray for any and everything that happens not only to them but to everyone of the world. Both Authors keep everyone in their prayers even people they don't know. Both Authors believe anyone can do anything through Christ.

Pray to be ok

Pray to be ok

Pray to be ok

Copyright © 2012 Author Name

All rights reserved.

ISBN: 978-0-578-31035-0

www.ingramcontent.com/pod-product-compliance
Lightning Source LLC
Chambersburg PA
CBHW020852090426
42736CB00008B/343